For _____

From _____

on _____

so that you will forever know
that you were born with eyes to
watch over you,
and hearts to always love you.

O SON OF BOUNTY!
Out of the wastes of nothingness,
with the clay of My command
I made thee to appear.
I destined for thee
eyes to watch over thee,
and hearts to love thee.
– Bahá'u'lláh

For a mother whose eyes always watched over
and whose heart loves forever. — M.P.

Written by Mona Parsa
Illustrations and cover art by Nidra N. Kilmer

www.AndSoYouWereBorn.com
www.facebook.com/AndSoYouWereBorn
www.twitter.com/AndSoUWereBorn

Printed in China
Library of Congress Control Number: 2012948647
ISBN: #978-0-9839047-0-0

For information about custom editions, special sales and bulk purchases, please contact
Twin Peacocks Publishing at contact@andsoyouwereborn.com.

# AND SO YOU WERE BORN

BY MONA PARSA

ILLUSTRATED BY

NIDRA N. KILMER

TWIN PEACOCKS PUBLISHING

CALIFORNIA

You are loved

and so you were born.

God brought you life,
protecting you and
guiding you

so you can shed forth His light.

You are loved

and so you were born.

God wishes for you to shine

and dazzle bright.

You are loved

and so you were born.

The people you love
watch over you **always,**

and say prayers with you
every night.

You are loved

and so you were born.

Your family and friends
are happy to see
that as you are growing
you show many virtues,

and are living so joyfully!

On the day of your birth,
every year you can say,

that you have grown and
become one year older,
on that splendid,
cheerful day!

Then you can show more
to your family and friends,
that you are
helpful,
      caring,
            and considerate,

just as a child of God would be.

Then you can show more,
to those who you love,
how much you've grown,
as then you'll be able to say
prayers without any help,

all on your very own.

Then you can show more
that you can dazzle bright,
just like God wishes for you to.
A heart like an illumined lamp,
and a life like a star

shining forth all of its light.

Then you can show more
that you can spread God's love
anywhere and everywhere you go,

and to anyone and
all who you know!

Children are a gift from the heavens. – Native American

Children are the world's most valuable resource and its best hope for the future. – John F. Kennedy

All works of love are works of peace. – Mother Theresa

What a grand thing, to be loved! What a grander thing still, to love! – Victor Hugo

Thou art like me, O well-speaking, well-thinking, well-acting youth, devoted to the good law, so in greatness, goodness, and beauty as I appear to thee. – **Zoroastrianism**

Arise, awake and acquire knowledge of God. – **Hinduism**

These are the various children, Laymen with faith and with virtue, Will shine bright amongst the people Like the moon released from the clouds. – **Buddhism**

How can I be useful, of what service can I be?
There is something inside me, what can it be?
– Vincent Van Gogh

Kind words will unlock an iron door. – Turkish Proverb

So wonderfully you made me,
wonderful are your works!
**– Christianity**

O God, guide me, protect me, make of me a shining lamp
and a brilliant star. Thou art the Mighty and the Powerful.
**– Bahá'í**

I have loved thee with an everlasting love;
therefore with affection
have I drawn thee.
**– Judaism**

He loves them and they love Him.
**– Islam**